There's a Bug in My Ear!

by Cynthia Amoroso ★ illustrated by Mernie Gallagher-Cole

Wonder Books

An Imprint of The Child's World®

childsworld.com

Published by The Child's World®
800-599-READ • childsworld.com

ISBN Information
9781503865556 (Reinforced Library Binding)
9781503866034 (Portable Document Format)
9781503866874 (Online Multi-user eBook)
9781503867710 (Electronic Publication)

LCCN 2022939530

Printed in the United States of America

ABOUT THE AUTHOR

As a daughter of elementary and English teachers, Cynthia Amoroso grew up in a home that was filled with language. She spent many hours enjoying reading and writing. Later, she followed in the footsteps of both her parents and became a teacher. As a high school English teacher and as an elementary teacher, Cynthia shared her love of language with students. She has always been fascinated with idioms and other figures of speech as they reflect and represent the culture and people who use them.

ABOUT THE ILLUSTRATOR

Mernie Gallagher-Cole lives in Pennsylvania with her husband and children. She uses idioms like the ones in this book every day. She has illustrated many children's books as well as greeting cards, puzzles, and games.

Contents

People use **idioms** every day. These are sayings and phrases with meanings that are different from the actual words. Some idioms seem silly. Many of them don't make much sense . . . at first.

This book will help you understand some of the most common idioms. The illustrations will show you how you might hear a saying or phrase. And the accompanying examples and definitions will tell you how the idiom is used, what it really means, and where it **originated**. All of these idioms—even the silly or humorous ones—are a rich, colorful part of the English language. You'll soon see that understanding idioms and knowing how to use them is a piece of cake!

Ants in your pants

It was Friday. Alberto was excited for the weekend. It was his birthday, and he was having a big party. That was all he could think about. Alberto couldn't sit still. He kept getting up and walking around. He had so much energy!

"Alberto!" exclaimed Mr. Baker, his teacher. "What's the matter today? You've got ants in your pants!"

MEANING: *To have a lot of energy; to have trouble staying still.*

ORIGIN: *The exact origin is unknown, but the phrase likely started in a **literal** sense. If an ant or other insect crawled into your clothing, you would find yourself squirming around and unable to stand still. You'd start moving quickly to remove it!*

At the end of my rope

It had been a long day for Uncle Jim. His car ran out of gas. The dog ran away. He tripped while he was walking home. Finally he reached his front door. "I'm at the end of my rope today!" he said to himself.

MEANING: *You just can't take any more! You have no more energy to deal with things that are happening.*
ORIGIN: *The* **expression** *most likely started with an actual rope—you've run out of rope to finish your work, whether you're climbing a mountain or tying up something. The phrase may also have originally referred to a farm animal tied to a rope and the limited area in which the animal could roam.*

Bee in your bonnet

"Amanda, if I hear you beg for a puppy one more time, I'll lose my temper!" Dad said with a scowl. "The answer is no. Don't bug me about it anymore!"

"What's the matter?" asked Mom as she walked into the room.

"Amanda's got a bee in her bonnet about getting a puppy," answered Dad.

MEANING: *To have an idea that you just can't forget about*
ORIGIN: *The phrase "to have a head full of bees" first appeared in the 1500s and became popular when the slightly altered "a bee in one's bonnet" appeared in a poem. You wouldn't be able to think of anything else if a bee were buzzing around in your hat!*

Bug in your ear

Marty and Dad were talking about summer vacation. "This year let's take a trip to the beach!" said Marty.

"That would be fun," agreed Dad. "I'd love to swim in the ocean."

"How about Mom?" asked Marty. "Do you think she would like a beach vacation too?"

"Tell you what," replied Dad. "I'll put a bug in her ear. We'll see if we can get her to start thinking about it."

MEANING: *To give someone an idea or to put an idea in someone's head*

ORIGIN: *This phrase likely came from the expression "to put a flea in one's ear," which comes from a French phrase that also means "to insert an **irresistible** notion."*

Cut to the chase

Daniel had been listening to Amy for ten minutes. He had wanted to hear all about the game, but he was losing interest. Amy was taking so long to tell the story. Finally, he couldn't listen any longer.

"Amy," moaned Daniel. "This is the longest story I've ever heard! Cut to the chase—did we win or lose?"

MEANING: *To get to the point, just say what you mean*
ORIGIN: *This saying can be traced to the Hollywood movie industry. The first movies made were silent films in the 1920s, and audiences enjoyed the action or chase scenes over the talking scenes, which could be boring. During editing, filmmakers would remove lengthy* **dialogue** *so they could get to, or cut to, the chase scenes.*

Feather your own nest

Kylie was excited because Mom and Dad were getting new furniture. She couldn't wait to move their old furniture into her room! She ran downstairs to ask Dad when it could all happen.

"What do you mean?" asked Dad. "You and your sister need to share that furniture. You can't have it all. You're feathering your own nest and not thinking about your sister!"

MEANING: *To only think of yourself; to get items, opportunities, or money for yourself without thinking of others' needs*
ORIGIN: *This saying has been in use since the 1500s. Birds line their nests with feathers to make them soft, comfortable homes.*

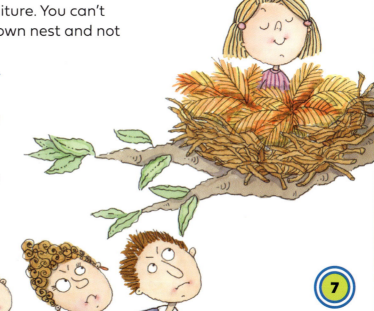

A fly in the ointment

Everything was ready for the party. The balloons were tied with pretty string. The music was playing. The cake was on the counter with the candles ready to be lit. Sophie was so excited! Now the guests could arrive. Suddenly there was a crash in the kitchen.

Sophie ran to see what had happened. There was her dog, licking cake and frosting from the floor. The dog had knocked over the cake! What would Sophie do now?

"Can you believe it?" exclaimed Mom. "I knew there would be a fly in the ointment today!"

MEANING: *Something that goes wrong when everything else is in place or is good*
ORIGIN: *Finding an insect in your ointment (a creamy substance for healing skin) would ruin it. This saying comes from the Old Testament of the Bible.*

Get up on the wrong side of the bed

Justin was eating breakfast when his sister, Jenna, came downstairs.

Jenna stomped into the kitchen. She yelled at the dog, made a face at Justin, and slammed the refrigerator door after grabbing some juice.

"What's the matter, Jenna?" asked Justin.

"Just leave me alone!" Jenna said, scowling.

"Wow! Did you get up on the wrong side of the bed this morning!" exclaimed Justin.

MEANING: *To be in a bad mood or to be crabby*

ORIGIN: *Superstitious beliefs were common in ancient times, and many people believed that anything on the left side was evil or bad. Ancient Romans had thought that putting your left foot down first when getting out of bed was bad luck!*

Green with envy

"This is so cool!" exclaimed Paul. "I've been wanting this new bike for months!"

"I'm glad you like it," said Mom. "I know you've worked hard to save your money. Are you going to let your brother try it out when we get home? You know he'll be green with envy!"

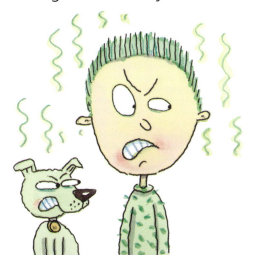

MEANING: *To be very jealous; to want something that someone else has*

ORIGIN: *This saying is credited to the playwright and poet William Shakespeare. In one of his works, he referred to jealousy as "the green sickness."*

Keep your chin up

Nina was heartbroken. Her dog had been gone since morning. She was very worried.

"Come on, Nina," said Dad. "Keep your chin up. We'll keep looking for Sniffles. He knows the neighborhood. I'm sure he's just having fun with some of the kids."

MEANING: *To stay happy or positive, even if it's hard*
ORIGIN: *Americans started using this expression in the early 1900s, and it's similar in meaning to the British phrase "keep a stiff upper lip." Keeping your chin up means that your head is held up and you are looking straight ahead. You are* **confident** *and ready.*

Loaded for bear

Mr. Seagram, Martin's next-door neighbor, had not been happy with Martin and his friends for a long time. They were always doing something to annoy him. Today one of the boys had hit a golf ball into Mr. Seagram's window. Mr. Seagram called Martin's dad.

"Was Mr. Seagram really mad?" Martin asked his father.

"Well, he was certainly loaded for bear when he called. I think he settled down a little by the time we finished talking," answered his dad. "But we need to talk about how you and your friends can be more respectful of Mr. Seagram and his home."

MEANING: *To be very angry or to be ready to take on a tough fight or argument*
ORIGIN: *This phrase was first used in North America in the 1800s. Its meaning originated from the literal sense; in other words, you have a loaded firearm with enough power to kill a bear.*

Many happy returns

Gina was having a great birthday. Her grandparents, aunts, uncles, and cousins were at her house. Everyone played games, laughed together, and enjoyed being with one another. Soon it was time for everyone to go home.

"Happy birthday, Gina! Many happy returns!" Grandma said as she gave Gina a big hug.

"Thank you, Grandma," replied Gina. "This was the best day! It was so much fun."

MEANING: *That you will have more happy days just like this one*

ORIGIN: *This phrase has been in use since the 1700s. The original expression was longer and served as a greeting: "many happy returns of the day."*

Mum's the word!

Aaron heard the back door open and close.

"Dad?" asked Aaron. "Is that you?" No one answered. Then Aaron saw Dad tiptoe around the corner. He was holding a huge bouquet of flowers.

"Whoa!" exclaimed Aaron. "Who gets those?"

"Shhh! They're for Mom," whispered Dad. "I'm going to hide them downstairs right now. I want to surprise her after dinner, so please don't tell her. Mum's the word!"

MEANING: *To keep a secret*

ORIGIN: *The word* mum *means "silent." This expression has been popular since the 1700s.*

Nose out of joint

Bryan was ignoring Marcus. Marcus had been elected captain of the team, and Bryan was jealous. Bryan had been sure he would be elected.

"Hey, Marcus!" exclaimed his friend Steven. "Where's Bryan? Why won't he walk home with us anymore?"

"Just forget about him for now," Marcus said and sighed. "His nose is out of joint. I'm hoping he'll be over it by next week. Let's go."

MEANING: *To act differently because you are mad or jealous*

ORIGIN: *This saying first appeared in England in the 1580s. If you were jealous or angry about something, those feelings may hurt as much as getting hit in the nose. (Interesting fact: A nose doesn't actually have a joint—it has* **cartilage**!*)*

On the tip of your tongue

Hannah answered the phone.

"Hello, Hannah," said her mom's friend Brenda. "Would you please ask your mom which lawn care company comes to your house? I want them to come to our house, too."

Hannah asked her mom. "Hmm. It's on the tip of my tongue," she replied. "Tell Brenda I'll call her back when I think of the company's name."

MEANING: *To have trouble remembering information that you know; to be ready to say something but not able to remember it exactly*

ORIGIN: *First appearing in a British novel in the 1700s, the expression became widely used by the mid-1800s.*

Out of touch

It had been a long weekend. Ann's parents had gone out of town, and her grandma had stayed with Ann and her brother.

"How was your weekend?" asked Dad when he got home.

"Terrible!" answered Ann. "We couldn't do anything. Grandma was afraid we'd break the computer so we couldn't use it. All we could watch on TV were little kids' shows. We couldn't have any ice cream or sweets for snacks. We were in bed by eight o'clock!" complained Ann. "It was miserable. Grandma is so out of touch!"

MEANING: *To have a gap in information or understanding; not to be clear on what's going on*

ORIGIN: *Many believe this phrase appeared around the late 1800s, and it refers to actual physical contact. Older musicians, for example, may have difficulty precisely touching or plucking the strings of an instrument compared to when they were much younger.*

Pass with flying colors

Sophie had been struggling in English class. To do better, she got extra help from Mr. Chavez after class. This morning there had been a big test. Sophie was very worried about how she had done. After school, she went to see Mr. Chavez.

"Mr. Chavez," Sophie said quietly. "Have you corrected my test yet? Could you please tell me how I did?"

"Yes," replied Mr. Chavez. "I've corrected your test, Sophie. You passed with flying colors. Well done!"

MEANING: *To do something very well, or to do it much better than you had to*
ORIGIN: *"Flying colors" first referred to naval ships coming to port, with their colorful flags waving from the ship's mast. It stood for a* **triumphant** *return and successful endeavor.*

The pot calling the kettle black

Marnie always had to be first. She always wanted the best things. She had to pick first. She had to be first in line. She wanted the biggest cookie or the best piece of cake. One morning, her brother Brett beat her to the kitchen. Mom had just gotten doughnuts from the bakery. Brett took the biggest doughnut with the most frosting.

"Mom!" called Marnie. "Tell Brett to put that doughnut back. He took the best one. He's being selfish."

"Well," said Mom, "isn't that the pot calling the kettle black?"

MEANING: *When a person acts one way and complains about another person acting the same way*

ORIGIN: *The phrase goes back to the early 1600s when people prepared meals over an open fire. A pot and a kettle were both dark in color—blackened by smoke from sitting over flames for long periods of time.*

Rings a bell

"Hello, everyone!" called Dad. He had just gotten home from a business trip. "I met someone you knew a long time ago," he said to Mom. "But she didn't know if you would remember her." He told Mom a story about a woman he'd met in a meeting.

"Hmm," Mom responded. "I'm not remembering her, but her name does seem to ring a bell."

MEANING: *To sound familiar as if you know something about it, but don't remember details*

ORIGIN: *This expression originated in the United States in the early 1900s. During that time, bells were often used to help people remember to do something or go somewhere.*

Sitting in the catbird seat

Tryouts for the traveling basketball team were today. Allison had been practicing for weeks. Her jump shot was great. She rarely missed a free throw. She was even hitting three-point baskets!

"Good luck, Allison," Dad said as she got out of the car. "You've worked hard for this. I'd say you're in the catbird seat!"

MEANING: *To be in good shape or to be in control*

ORIGIN: *A catbird, which got its name because it sounds like the meows of cat, sits high up in trees where it has the best view of its prey. The phrase first appeared in the 1800s in the southern United States.*

Take it with a grain of salt

Sonia was upset. She'd worked very hard on her solo for the school concert. Today she had to miss practice. After school, Sonia's classmate Eva told her that the solo wasn't being included in the program.

"Well, Sonia," sighed her mom after hearing what had happened. "Eva has told you many things in the past that haven't ended up being true. If I were you, I think I'd take Eva's news with a grain of salt. You should talk to your choir teacher tomorrow."

MEANING: *To question something you've been told or not to completely believe something you hear*

ORIGIN: *Some believe this expression was first created by ancient Romans, referring to an* **antidote** *for poison. The saying became popular in the mid-1600s.*

Tip of the iceberg

Mom knew that Laura and her best friend, Kristin, weren't getting along. It had been going on for weeks. All Mom knew was that Kristin was upset.

"Laura, why don't you tell me why Kristin is so angry with you," suggested Mom. "Maybe I can help."

After Laura explained, Mom left the room, thinking that Kristin had no reason to be so angry with Laura. What Mom didn't know was that there was more to the story. Laura's explanation was just the tip of the iceberg.

MEANING: *To hear, see, or know only part of something that is much bigger*
ORIGIN: *The saying, which became popular in the 1900s, refers to the fact that most of an iceberg (about 90 percent) is not visible—it is below the surface of the ocean.*

Under the weather

Stella was hungry. It was Saturday, and every Saturday her mother made waffles for breakfast. But today Mom was late. Stella went upstairs to see what her mom was doing. She opened her mother's bedroom door and saw that she was still in bed.

"I'm sorry, honey," replied her mom. "I'm feeling a little under the weather this morning. I think I need to get some extra sleep today."

MEANING: *To feel sick*

ORIGIN: *This saying originated in the 1700s in the United States. It was a time when people often traveled by boat. In bad weather the sea would be rough, causing many to get seasick. People referred to the condition as "suffering under the influence of the bad weather," which was eventually shortened to "under the weather."*

Where there's smoke there's fire

Toby was helping Grandma bake brownies for her party. After the brownies cooled, Grandma and Toby cut them into squares. They packed them into a big box for the party. A little later, Grandma went to put a few more brownies in the box. She saw that half of the brownies were gone!

"Toby!" called Grandma. "Do you know what happened to the brownies?"

Toby came around the corner. There was chocolate smudged around his lips. He had crumbs on his shirt, too. Grandma knew exactly what had happened to the missing brownies.

"Oh, Toby. Where there's smoke, there's fire. I think you do know where the brownies went!" exclaimed Grandma.

MEANING: *There are clues that something has happened or that there is a problem*

ORIGIN: *The saying has been in use since ancient times and became popular in the mid-1500s. Where there is fire, there is smoke. In this sense, smoke* **symbolizes** *the clues to whatever the "fire" might be.*

Glossary

antidote (AN-tee-doht): Something used to reverse or prevent the effects of poison.

cartilage (KAR-tuh-lij): Flexible connective tissue found in many areas of the body.

confident (KON-fih-dent): Feeling sure about something, having trust or faith.

dialogue (DYE-uh-log): A conversation between two or more people; a discussion.

expression (ek-SPREH-shun): A common saying; telling or showing your thoughts and feelings.

familiar (fuh-MIL-yur): Easily recognized or known by many people.

idioms (ID-ee-umz): Phrases or sayings whose meaning can't be understood by their individual words taken separately.

irresistible (eer-ih-ZIH-stuh-bul): Impossible to resist.

literal (LIT-er-uhl): Concerned with the facts and free from exaggeration; exact.

originated (uh-RIJ-ih-nay-ted): To bring or come into being; to begin.

superstitious (soo-pur-STIH-shus): Relating to superstition, which refers to a belief or practice that isn't grounded in facts; trust in magic or chance.

symbolizes (SIM-buh-lye-zez): To serve as a symbol of; to stand for something.

triumphant (try-UHM-funt): Successful; celebrating a victory.

Wonder More

- Write a short story using an idiom. You can make up a story or use an experience from your own life. For example, if you choose the idiom "every cloud has a silver lining," you could write about discovering something good in an otherwise bad situation.

- In what ways do idioms impact our writing? In your opinion, do they help improve our ability to tell stories and describe events, or are they unnecessary? Explain your reasoning.

- Think of an idiom that isn't in this book and create a new entry. Write your own brief story using the idiom, and draw a picture to go with it. Then write down its meaning and origin. If you don't know the idiom's origin, where could you learn more about it?

- The idioms "green with envy" and "nose out of joint" from this book have similar meanings. In what ways are they different? Write down your own examples for each one.

Find Out More

In the Library

Heinrichs, Ann. *Similes and Metaphors*. Mankato, MN: The Child's World, 2020.

Pearson, Yvonne, and Mernie Gallagher-Cole (illustrator). *Rev Up Your Writing in Fictional Stories*. Mankato, MN: The Child's World, 2016.

Schubert, Susan, and Raquel Bonita (illustrator). *I'll Believe You When . . . Unbelievable Idioms from around the World*. Minneapolis, MN: Lerner, 2020.

Zafarris, Jess. *Once Upon a Word: A Word-Origin Dictionary for Kids*. Emeryville, CA: Rockridge Press, 2020.

On the Web

Visit our website for links about idioms: **childsworld.com/links**

Note to Parents, Caregivers, Teachers, and Librarians: We routinely verify our Web links to make sure they are safe and active sites. So encourage your readers to check them out!

~~~~~~~

Index